backwards days

also by stuart dischell

Dig Safe
Evenings & Avenues
Good Hope Road
Animate Earth

backwards days

stuart dischell

penguin poets

PENGUIN BOOKS

Published by the Penguin Group
Penguin Group (USA) Inc.,
375 Hudson Street, New York, New York 10014, U.S.A.
Penguin Group (Canada), 90 Eglinton Avenue East, Suite 700, Toronto,
Ontario, Canada M4P 2Y3 (a division of Pearson Penguin Canada Inc.)
Penguin Books Ltd, 80 Strand, London WC2R 0RL, England
Penguin Ireland, 25 St Stephen's Green, Dublin 2, Ireland
(a division of Penguin Books Ltd)
Penguin Group (Australia), 250 Camberwell Road, Camberwell, Victoria
3124, Australia (a division of Pearson Australia Group Pty Ltd)
Penguin Books India Pvt Ltd, 11 Community Centre, Panchsheel Park,
New Delhi – 110 017, India
Penguin Group (NZ), 67 Apollo Drive, Rosedale, North Shore 0632,
New Zealand (a division of Pearson New Zealand Ltd.)
Penguin Books (South Africa) (Pty) Ltd, 24 Sturdee Avenue, Rosebank,
Johannesburg 2196, South Africa

Penguin Books Ltd, Registered Offices:
80 Strand, London WC2R 0RL, England

First published in Penguin Books 2007

Page ix constitutes an extension of this copyright page.

ISBN 978-0-14-311255-6
CIP data available

Set in Janson
Designed by Ginger Legato

147204767

for my teachers

Acknowledgments

Certain of these poems, sometimes in different versions or under other titles, first appeared in the publications to which my grateful acknowledgment is made: *Agni*: "House and Highway," "While an Old Clock Rang the Hour," and "You"; *Cave Wall*: "From a Long Way Off," "The Hungry Hour," and "Three Addresses"; *Chattahoochee Review*: "Psychological Poem" and "Elegy Without a Name"; *Forklift, Ohio*: "Relentless Soliloquy" and "Song of the Night"; *Greensboro News and Record*: "To a Compass Rose"; *Hayden's Ferry Review*: "Karma from Scratch" and "Krakow"; *Kenyon Review*: "Backwards Days" and "This Time in the Sky"; *Naked Punch* (UK): "Well Till He, Too, Fell Ill"; *Roger*: "In Polynesia"; *storySouth*: "Everywhere the Desert Met the Wind," "Heaven Was Elsewhere," "The Interrupted Sleep of Skeletons," and "Later There Were Swans"; *Terminus*: "A Week of Rain in my Republic," "Death Perception," "In the Manner of SD," "Lyric Poet Disease," and "Tale of the Garrett"; *Verb*: "Unsung" and "Lively in the Twilight with Abandoning Fleas"; *Washington Square Review*: "A Signal."

"She Put on Her Lipstick in the Dark" first appeared in *The Atlantic*.

"Around the Corner" contains a translation and variation of "Autumn" by Guillaume Apollinaire. In "Shanty," *When will I see you again* is a lyric from "A Man Needs a Maid" by Neil Young. "The Laugh of the Thief" is titled after a phrase used by Martin Arnold. "In Corcovado" refers to a song written by Antonio Carlos Jobim and Gene Lees: "Corcovado (Quiet Nights of Quiet Stars)." My thanks to the John Simon Guggenheim Memorial Foundation and the University of North Carolina at Greensboro for their support during the time in which I wrote these poems.

"I got *everything* wrong.
I did not get one single thing right."

Randall Jarrell
The Truth

Contents

backwards days

Behind the bookcase is a balled-up tissue
A safety pin and the fur of a now dead cat
(I don't think I will clone him)
There is a price tag for parts
And a key to my old apartment (hello!)
This is the birthplace of sneezes
The depository of receipts
Condom wrappers (yippee)
And coins coins coins coins
Here is a ticket stub from the ball game
(Row HH) a quote from a roofer
The business card of a dwarf
(My father had me shake his hand
At the side show) three bobby pins
A toothpick a suit button
Here lies a pen with a lady
(She's naked upside down)
Mold resembling a fruit peel
A postcard of the Rockies
(How's the weather down there?)
An aspirin and a root beer barrel
And a matchbook with a number
(I did not write the name)
To start a fire

Out on the leaf-blown yard where the wind has made a skirmish
In the leaves, where the red and yellow and yellow and red
Have arranged themselves in momentary heaps like drifts

Of snow on the right and left of the yard still mostly green,
Where each caught leaf behind the drainpipe running down
From the eaves, each on the lawn appears slick as fresh paint

After rain. On the pathway, points down, three maple leaves
Scatter in the noon already too cold, where the shadows
Of the trees cross this path, the fieldstone wide, the mortar flecked,

The little mosses retreated to the shade, the mosses nearly black
Smudges in a tangle of roots. The mosses live to the side
Of each heel print, the scuff of brooms and mowers and the rake

Now leaned against a red oak trunk. The pathway
Leads up three brick steps to the porch. The black iron railing
Whose underside needs repainting is attached to the brickwork

At its base. Two cement urns stand at each side of the red door
In which six thick small panes are framed. The door has a mail slot
On a spring. It opens three quarters of the way. Daylight

Illuminates part of the floor and the letters on the wide boards.
The brass handle of the door turns with great effort, the lock
And wrist click. The edge where the mechanism is concealed

Contains two brass buttons, the jutting tongue of the latch, the flat
Heads of four three-inch Phillips head screws, the company name,
And the retracted bolt echoing in the hall (is that you?).

The house was old, the floors were crooked.
A marble rolled several ways before stopping.
One hallway led to nothing but a window
At the edge of the city, near the highway

Where a dog was always crossing
The median in the rain. Under the overpass
Two men sitting up in sleeping bags
Passed a bottle while a third
Grilled dinner on a wire shelf rigged
Across a fruit bin salvaged from
A junked refrigerator. The clever one,
He knew the collection schedules,
Assembled his office among the pigeons,
Bookcases and a desk and chair
He had gotten the others to carry
Down the embankment. He was the one
Who found the money taped under the drawer,
The one who looked for such things
That bought the chicken, bread, and beer
And the spirits the others were drinking
Toasting the success of their leader
After he swallowed half the bottle.

In the front yard the lawn needs mowing.
There's a well choked with weeds.
The rusted bell without its tongue
Can still be sounded with a stone.

There was a fistfight around the corner just breaking
Up and one boy said my dad was in it, but it was over
By the time I came around the corner. My dad by then
Was rolling down his shirtsleeves and I could not see
The other man if there was one because I no longer
Remember if what I saw or heard was true because
My dad said it never happened. He may be right
I may have dreamed his glasses in his shirt pocket,
His bleeding knuckles because I wanted it to happen
That my dad was the kind of man who got into fistfights
On his way home from work, that I would be that kind
Of man, too. Once I put a friend of mine in a headlock
Outside a bowling alley. He drank a cup of piss
He thought was beer. He blamed me for not telling him
And tried to sock me in the mouth. I was glad the joke
Was not on me. He should not have been so eager to grab
The cup another friend pretended he was drinking—
I hit my friend in the face to keep him from squirming
And his glasses fell in a puddle of spit, and the friend
Who pissed in the cup laughed even more and nearly
Stepped on the glasses as I pressed my friend's neck
Down close to the sidewalk. Give? I told him, give.

While an Old Clock Rang the Hour

One evening early in the century
On streets familiar to the heart, I saw
Benches and light poles, rooftops and spires,
Bridges one after the other across
The river lit at the far end of its line, the red
Sun mixing the blue and green,
The thread of the river a fuse to my mood.

I was glad to be out of the little room,
The bed that filled it, the half moon
Of the table, the folding chair where
I ate bread and soup and wrote my notes
Concerning a person much like myself
At peace in a foreign city, perambulator
Of urban regions, seeker of elusive moments.

I wanted new friends and new music,
Dive bars at the edges of the city's core,
Places I could go alone and keep my jacket
On. I was dancing again inside my skin,
Having lasted through The Year
Of No Kisses, I smoked and drifted
Among people, listened to their inflected talk.

I thought of the friend who would not see me,
How her face had turned from mine,
That last expression she formed at the corner
Of her mouth. I remembered myself
At home in the mirror trying to get right
That little curve she made above her lip,
The scythe that cleared the wild flowers.

I recalled the mornings in my parents' house,
How they defended each other's health,
Their greetings at the breakfast table,
The rituals of coffee, fruit, and the paper—
The old quarrels gone, the villains now clear.
I sat with them and heard them say
"They are good today, the blueberries."

I pictured my children at play in the garden
Of their home in the town while I was still
In the picture, my wife's face under a wide-
brimmed straw hat, her sun blond hair,
The blue eyed look she used to give me
When I was worthy of being seen that way,
And the dog retrieving nothing for no one.

I passed the houseboats and barges
Docked along the banks, their interiors
Not yet illuminated, the gear on hooks,
The steering wheels, the alarm systems such
People keep on guard. I longed for
Other people's rooms, supper invitations,
And ways to save what was left of the money.

I watched the chimney pots get dark last,
The night filling in the spaces between the tiles.
I had seen it many times, knew the look of it
Without going out as I charted and dozed,
Nestled in the hollow of the mattress, the map
Across my chest, my breath rippling the lines and dashes,
The broken path to the star field ahead in the sky.

My son's teacher holds backwards days in class
Where the students come to school in pajamas,
Eat dessert for breakfast, say good night
When they mean good morning. So it is
I say good-bye to you because I hate you
And find you ugly and every moment with you
Is boring to me.
                    (How is it when I speak
These words I am stricken even though I am joking.
How is it I have come to say a word like *stricken*?)

Inky blossom
At the page corner
Like a sea creature
Yourself, an octopus
Of the cardinal and ordinal,
Empress of the measured world
You reign under the crown
Of a true north.
The wheel of your face
Is more perfect than the Earth
And suggestive of windblown journeys,
Thirty-two I believe in fact
Radiating in degrees
All pointing away from you,
Darling of each, sweetheart of none,
The map would be lost as the traveler.

Out west we lived in a view.
We could see forever was not far
Enough. The dinosaurs
Had walked across our valley.
You could see their footprints
Stuck in the mud.
Our volcano was extinct also.
Our mountains treeless.
Our slow-moving river sometimes dry.
(One evening we snuck out on the golf course
Near the rental house and I played the pennywhistle
And you and our daughter did a mouse dance
And a jackrabbit watched from behind a cactus
Where he thought we could not see him.)

They searched for us in high and low places,
Using bird calls, whistles, and their own
Voices. We heard but would not answer,
Did not really listen, we already knew
Others would mistake our fire for their own.
Who could blame them, sisters and brothers,
Long-distance ramblers who smelled our smoke
From a long way off? From the boulevards
They wandered, past the abandoned
Vehicles they had taken from the city,
Past the warehouses and factories, inter-
States and rail yards. They had been told
Of music beyond them but not of fire.

I

There was a bed, a window, and a sky.
The bed was the shoulder of a cloud.
The window was one among many
Along the highway. The sky kept changing.
We were naked, on top of the covers,
The bars of the blinds lit the threshold.

II

I saw her well-dressed along a busy street
Attracting everyone who passed, and one
Or two bumped into her at the crosswalk, the turnstile,
And a few stood too close on the train—
Men and women alike, whose fires were lit
By the fragrant oil she wears on her skin.

III

We were arm in arm under the double rows
Of the chestnut trees. Beyond our feet were the first
Farewell leaves. We were with friends we had
Not yet met. We kept bumping into each other
And being silly, having forgotten where it was
We were walking, but all of us were lit.

The cities were anonymous
The problems generic
And the people who lived
Out their lives did nothing
Remarkable. Most were
Afraid. They ate and drank.
They had babies or avoided them.
They prayed and kissed and sometimes forgot
Each other in the dark.
They did the basic human thing,
Knowing they would die
Following the leader
While cursing their wages.
(But once you and I did
Something specific, and a couple
Of people saw us later on the street.)

After work in the city on a spring evening
When I still wore shoes with leather soles
And an open expression on my face,
My tie was gorgeous, the open button
At my throat a little raffish, my thoughts
On the heel, energized and instrumental.

Clusters of notes hastened at the corners.
I did not see myself as anything much,
Eager to nod, whistle a tune, wave hello
To a merchant. I was not treacherous,
No place to rush to or anyone to fool.
No words interfered with that rhythm.

She Put on Her Lipstick in the Dark

I really did meet a blind girl in Paris once.
It was in the garden of a museum
Where I saw her touching the statues.
She had brown hair and an aquamarine scarf.

It was in the garden of the museum
I told her I was a thief disguised as a guard.
She had brown hair and an aquamarine scarf.
She told me she was a student from Grenoble.

I told her I was not a thief disguised as a guard.
We had coffee at the little commissary.
She said she had time till her train to Grenoble.
We talked about our supreme belief in art.

We had coffee at the little commissary
Then sat on a bench near the foundry.
We talked about our supreme belief in art.
She leaned her head upon my chest.

We kissed on a bench near the foundry.
I closed my eyes when no one was watching.
She leaned her head upon my chest.
The museum was closing. It was time to part.

I really did meet a blind girl in Paris once.
I never saw her again and she never saw me.
In a garden she touched the statues.
She put on her lipstick in the dark.

I close my eyes when no one is watching.
She had brown hair and an aquamarine scarf.
The museum was closing. It was time to part.
I never saw her again and she never saw me.

Yesterday I fell in love eleven times—
With my son's teacher, two joggers,
Three dog-walkers, the pharmacist's
New assistant, the latte girl at
The coffee shop, a Lesbian
Couple, and my ex-wife—
But today I did not fall in love at all.

Tomorrow I'm planning to marry—
I'm going to feast in the groves and kiss a tick,
I'm going to camp along a river/on a mountain
And build my own fire, I'm going
To ask out the latte girl with foam on her lips
And we will pitch a tent on a bed near the sea.

Share your shower with a leper

Give your eyes to science while you're still using them

Eat only fallen fruit or meat that's dropped on the floor

Clean gum off the bottoms of bus seats with your fingernails

Play hopscotch ahead of a platoon through a minefield

Will your life savings to the next telemarketer

Make a home in your jewel box for spiders

Resuscitate a dying porcupine

Forgive rich people the arrogance of their tailpipes

Shine the shoes of the indigent and indignant

Offer your attic to store atomic waste

Celebrate your fiftieth birthday cleaning public toilets

Learn foreign languages to help your enemies

There was a tumbleweed
Behind the house whispering
To his tall friend the cactus
About blue scat the wild dog made
About an hour after he ate
The child's Play-Doh rabbit,
Salty from her hands and the chemicals
Its color and texture were composed of—

And while the pair in the moonlight chortled,
The wild dog in the tall grass
Recounted to himself how the day
Began not badly, an overturned
Trash can by the rest stop,
A dove with a broken wing,
Slow lizards at noon, a windfall
Of chicken bones in a bag at dusk.
And maybe later in the half harvested field
Rats in the furrows when he felt better.

Whoever owns the brick house
On the river bank, I would like
Your study I see with the big
Windows and desk and shelves
Of books that all must be
Interesting to you. I think I could
Get some work done there also.
I could research a life in place
With something natural occurring
Outside the windows, a body
Of water in motion, seen through
A dozen panes of glass, each
A portrait of the river. I would look
Through your binoculars. I could
See your friends and forebears arrayed
In the dining room, the roast and bird
Upon the table—and the fellow I assume
Is your father, sleeves rolled to the elbows
Offering the end cut to your grandfather.
I would taste the blood of the beast,
The wild flavor of the game—
The wing and leg that were your portion,
What others believed you desired,
How you ate to the bone what was given
And awaited seconds, the gravy cooling
In the china pitcher. I would attend
The weddings and burials, mingle
Among bridesmaids and pallbearers,

Hear come cries and death rattles,
Know the children and their occupations,
Pore over your daily, weekly, and monthly
Earnings inscribed in your handwriting.
I would note your thrift and habits,
How it was you never squandered, the way
You managed your debts, borrowing
What you could return, working to credit
The family crest above the door,
Its emblem a river and shield.
I would stand where you stood, your shadow
Cast upon the lawn, the plantings
In bloom coloring the edges and hold
To the light the book you wrote
About the errors you made when you left
The world you studied in your study.

The people on the bus mean nothing to me now.
Their cares are like mine. Let them ride on.

I had the wish you are supposed to wish.
I had the prayer for the blind dead god.

Cash in my hand and a fish in my mouth,
I sailed over the broken ground.

What, did you see the treasure of my chest
Was ripped and de-doublooned?

Buried to my head in the tide
I swam through the well of my throat.

A man pulls an orange cat
In a wagon along the curb.
Garbage is their grocery and as they depart
The courtyards and dumpsters the orange cat
Meows a poem about a calf
And a crippled peasant who walk
Slowly through the autumn mist
That hides the dwellings of the poor.
And as they go, the man adds his verse
About a ring and a broken heart.

Autumn, autumn,
Summer has gone.
Two silhouettes
Pass in the mist.

It is Monday in the rue Christine
And through the door the sparse crowd
Outside the cinema has trouble
Lighting its cigarettes in the rain
And across the street I am telling
My friends over the music in the bar
It is Monday in the rue Christine
Just like the poem by Apollinaire
Who lived and died a couple
Of streets away I tell this to James
Making death's heads behind the bar
To Pauline when she comes back
From bussing tables and to the person
Seated beside me who happens to
Wash dishes on the rue Christine
And I tell him how Apollinaire died
Months after being shelled
At the front and to the best
Of my memory trepanned
Dying with a brow of bandages
In his rooms above the Place
A deep sorrow in his head
A statue of which hides in
The garden behind the Church

You asked me not to write
About the city anymore

Or the disturbed people I met
When I lived there—

But I thought of an apartment
In a wintry basement,

The sound of snow
Scraped off the first

Step of the stairs outside
The tall high window of the hall,

How after she left
I behaved like her,

How I slept two days straight
Trying out her medication.

The day that I found art in my first name
Was the same day I saw hell in my last.

There was a girl there, of course,—
Touching a wet finger
To a postage stamp,
Pursing her lips
On the double bed.

I went to kiss
The cat-tongue rough
Of her each bent knee.

I was weak then, not yet a liar.
One of us had said,
What we do is our own business.
Then we broke the windows
And looted the store.

This is the hour
Rings dissolve in liquor.

Each tide of the chorus is dangerous.
I keep my faith below the knuckle

And sing to you across the piano.
And to you, too.

I take off my blue and white striped shirt
And walk along the beach in just bikini bottoms
Because I am still a girl with a great ass
And have awakened in someone's sandy bed,
Having left my flip-flops along the shore
When the sun and tide were out,
Before the moon made green phosphor
Break from the waves, dolphins leap,
And the surfers on long boards cast
Their shadows' passage upon the sea.
When Astrud Gilberto sings
I return to our old room,
Pastel sheets on which we slept
Naked under the fan all day,
Oh how lovely.

She was telling him a story a friend told her
About a couple the friend had seen at a hotel
In Los Angeles. *It was nearly dawn.*
She had set her alarm and got up to call
New York when she looked through
The curtains she had opened partway
To see the numbers of the phone on the desk.
He had seen her friend once several years ago
In Houston when they lived in St. Paul. It was easy
For him to picture her standing by the desk
Feeling more formal talking business standing up
In a tee shirt and underpants. She did not seem
Like the kind of person who slept naked
When alone. She was from the suburbs of Chicago.
He had remembered her accent, the way she said
Coffee. She was pretty in her tennis dress.
There was a little sweat on her lip, but all business.
He could see the outline of her breast when she held
In the tips of her fingers the edge of the curtain.
They were all at a conference selling what they sold.
People from all over, Duluth, Wichita, Rapid City
When they worked the home district. He lay back
On the pillows. She took off her dress, told him,
She had just hung up the phone and started
To close the curtains when she saw a couple in the hotel
Pool, the little pool in the courtyard, not
The big pool with the bar you like. Indeed he knew

The hotel, the perfect blue water of the big pool
No one swam in, the comfortable thick pads
Of the lounge chairs, the expensive strong drinks,
The women with dogs in their purses, tanned legs,
The whole LA show. He had grown up in Boston,
His wife was from Denver. They met in college
In Philadelphia. They got married in Miami
Where her parents retired. His were buried
In their hometown of Portland. She went on,
She was closing the curtain when she saw them
On the rope across the shallow end of the pool,
A couple in the water, and the woman looked
Like she was sitting on a swing. He pictured them,
The man standing up, holding the woman under
The backs of her knees, her arms around his neck,
How the pressure of their weight would sink them
Below the waterline, *and soon her head was under the surface*
And every couple of minutes she gulped the air and
Pulled his face under and they were kissing there
Breathing each other's breath and she was scared
They might be drowning each other and whether
She should call the desk or go out there herself to save them.
Then they broke the surface slick as seals he imagined
And recalled the ones he had seen north of San Francisco.
And here was the thing, when they climbed out
Of the pool they did not kiss good-bye but went
Back to their separate rooms. He considered

Who they were to each other as if this were a parable.
Then the reasons why the friend might have told
This story to his wife and where it happened she told it.
And there was his wife unhooking her bra, the light on
Her shoulders from the bedside lamp beside her, clearing
Her throat as she always did at that moment so
He would not fail to see the loveliness of her skin.

A signal off
        A tower somewhere
Sent a signal
        To another tower
Somewhere until
        It reached you
And we were
        Voice to voice
Below the orbiting
        Satellites, I
In the parking lot
        And you by the sea—
Imagine Guinevere
        And Lancelot
Mobile to mobile
        Talking across the
Sword between them
        Or Abelard dialing
Heloise whose phone
        Was set to vibrate,
There's voice mail
        From Orpheus
And one dropped call,
        Echo's message was
Always the same,
        Iseulte's too—

But it suited us
        Those nights we held
Each other's voices,
        Heroes then, not cheats.

sips from the hollows
of your collarbones

where the water collects
after you wash your hair

and the comb has run through it
(quick like a roe in the meadow)

once or twice in the sun, blinking
on the porch before your shift

Just as they were
Ever together
So he remains
Solitary forever
In the days apart
Cancelled on the calendar
Another x in the shipwrecked's log.

"Rain and the cliffs were invisible.
        Along the reef dolphin fins
                Took shape in the storm.
        If you are looking for me
                Give me sails on the horizon,
        And I will signal from the lagoon
News of my survival."

She said there was no more to say. We kept on
Anyway, trying to tow the mother
Ship off the shoals of August
Where it had stalled when the wind failed.

We had parted well, the moon was new,
We said good-bye in my car near the harbor.
I kissed her eyes and ears and chin and brow.
She was off to work and I was driving home.

And I was going fast talking to her on the phone
And I sang *When will I see you again.*
And I did not know the answer and got all anxious
And we got cut off in a region of lost signals.

Because we do not have memories
I have invented one in which we are

In Polynesia. You are paddling the canoe
And I am taking your picture because when

I cannot touch you I take your picture.
The funny thing is how we discover

What else was with us in the water,
How we did not see it on the surface

And you did not have to tell it
Leave us alone because we are in love.

In the photograph the village leader
Wears a hat on the beach like the one
My grandfather wore in the photograph
On Mother's dresser. Where the chief got it,
If it floated on the tide or if he took it off
An unknown explorer no one can tell.
(Did I say my grandfather drowned
In a lagoon while hunting wild canaries
Near Rockaway Beach outside New York City?
Did I say he too was otherwise naked?)

Don't step on the broken glass of the future,
My barefoot darlings.

A broom cannot sweep away tears.

The animals in your fables are real,
Look around you.

If asked always say you have been there before.

Once I stayed in an apartment that had no windows,
Only skylights that were opaque except for the outlines
Of the feet of the pigeons roosting under the eaves—
Filthy birds I avoided them on the streets, the narrow ones
They chose and clotted. I avoided them as I did certain dogs
In doorways or the disreputable proprietors who allowed
Unsavory people to congregate outside their businesses.
I was alone and lived in fear. I could not look up or out
And down was the floor. One day while blackening my shoes
While wearing them, I stumbled on the laces and the rag smeared
A line of polish on the wall. When I tried to clean it with a sponge,
It lengthened. I drew back. Inspired, I made the outline
Of a window, two big boxlike panes of glass and started
To fill them with lighter motion. Each day after my labors
In the globe factory, I would climb the six flights
To my apartment, eat my supper, and with the back end
Of a spoon scratch away at the frame and sill. It was just
Idle movement at first, the metal working through the papered
Layers. I pictured the sun spilling on the rug at breakfasttime,
Starlight over the city. I bought a hammer and broke
The plaster. I bought a saw and cut out the lathing.
When I got to the bricks, I bought a chisel and chipped
The mortar. All that was left was pushing the first one at night.
My apartment was at the rear of the building. I pictured
The courtyard with its stunted trees, the bicycles and strollers
The tenants would keep there, the hose the janitor used
To wash out the trash cans. I tried to push it through,
But it would not budge. I bought a crowbar and pried it out.

No air, no wind. I slipped my hand in and my fingers
Stopped at another layer. Enough I said. I bought a sledgehammer
And a radio. I stripped to my waist and broke the wall down
After four strong blows and when the bricks stopped falling
I saw there was no sky or courtyard, but a roomful of dust
Where the children had slept, three in the bed with the night-light on.

I am not a real person
And the days I lived in never

Happened, yet they were all I had.
I left my dent in the landscape

And my marker,
But I was never really here.

I'm a death's head, a loser
Without a heart

In the landscape,
Born in the shit of this world.

She was a one-eyed girl
Wild in some games

She won in the evening
But lost by the morning

Because she still cared
About her mom and dad

Sent them twenties in the mail
To the old country of New Jersey

Told me she dreamed of being shot
In the head more than once

Said she remembered
How entering her brain the second

Shot felt like nothing going through her.
She took another slug of vodka.

I laughed. She laughed.
Then there was the vodka.

Nothing so funny there.
Afterward the light was not white but clear.

Like a bone buried in my heart's yard
Forgotten two decades or more,
Your slender self has disinterred there,
Causing me to bay from atop my shoulders
At the rind of moon the sky scribbled its number
Upon leaving the party.
                              Making the rounds
Of former haunts I scare you up
In fishnets and a leather skirt at
A warehouse dance club in an industrial
District of the city, the dragon not yet
Broken in your skin, the stud like a pearl
Un-pierced in your tongue, the Chinese
Character for heat not yet written
At the base of your spine, the collected
Pills that made dead planets of your eyes
Not yet swallowed, the genies of
Drinks still captured in their bottles,
A caviar of your eggs hidden
In your guts . . .
                              Yet it was possible
For you to look and act suburban,
Designer emblems on man-made fibers,
Three shelves of cosmetics and school trophies,
The indistinct faces glazed on the bureau,
Out the window the cables of the bridge

And the river, you said, that kept us honest.
Smoking before breakfast, we watched Saturday
Cartoons under the blankets, your wake-up on the
Nightstand, the rabbit ears on the tv winged with foil.

Of the Shoe

The streets have gotten to me again.
I'm tapping along the paved way.
Take me to the cobbler, my old friend,
See if he can fix us up again.

Of the Station

Past the terminal of small animals
Something has gotten under my skin.
A window opens in my forehead,
In both pupils the oncoming train.

Of the Night

Through the fog I think the lantern
That hangs from the back of the wagon
Moving steadily ahead of me
Forever is the light of my home.

Relatives gave him a tortoiseshell kitten
So his days alone would seem less so
And give his place a girlish presence
When he returned from work and visits
With friends who said little until he left.
Poor man. The fur made him sneeze.
Strands of it clung to his suits, the house
Took on a sharpish smell, and his eyes
Acquired the color red. All agreed
He seemed run-down. But he never
Drank. But he never smoked.
And strayed but once with a holiday kiss.
Days of ritual and small gestures
With the added expense of cat food.

I think the sun should go down, it's been light enough.
There are too many ambulatory shadows.
I should close my eyes and reduce their number.
Shadows live in the half light.
They are good only for guessing the time.
They stretch the truth, their movements exaggerate
The postures and gestures of normal people.
Night will gather them in ancient temples.
Night will shield them under leather wings.
The shadows will not be given back their songs.
Like stone, part of me is cold to the touch.

They Said It Happened, Maybe It Did

He was looking at her breasts
And the china blue veins
Where the spiders ran through her skin.
She was indeed a naked person.

O map uncharted
Of the heart's survey,
World in a drop.
Compass needle spinning.

Your eyes are gone and nearly
All we knew of the city,
Its graveyards and walls,
The spires, domes, and towers,
Its little incorporated villages
(Only their names survive),
The lane where your parents lived,
Your musical uncles, the sitting room,
The bowl of asters on the table.
How we listened to your father
Play his compositions. After dinner
We walked through the scattered
Blossoms of the chestnut trees.
You were older in that house
Among the books, the candlesticks,
Your mother's perpetual illness,
Your father's gambling losses.
We kissed in the arbor
And you were such a girl
I did not kiss you again
Until our wedding day. A carriage
Led that procession, too.

On the Ground and Through the Clouds

On this side of Security
Not wanting to go further,
I sat on a bench and sent a text
On my cell. The weather
Was unspeakable, rain
In great efforts. You texted
Back, "Have a safe trip home."
But to fly home was not possible.
You should have known that
The plane would be delayed
And there no longer was a home
For me to speak of, certainly
Not my dogless rooms
On Howard Street.

I could not bring myself to drag
My suitcase across the polished
Floor to check in, wait in line,
Take off my jacket, belt, and shoes
And show my ticket and license.
You should have known that
To board the flight *home*
Meant starting again the engine
Of longing, the wheels and gauges,
Mixed and missed signals, the calibration
Of last night's quarrel, our hungover
Words, the jet fuel of lost time,
And the vague memory of six

Bison heads gazing through
The hotel room window
From the facade across the street.

I dialed a friend who said, "Go
Board your flight," and I did
What he said and the things I said
I would not do, walked through
The airport to my plane
And its unlikely on-time departure,
Its rising through the black and white
Of the rained-on city, and I tried not to
Picture where you live with your boyfriend,
The one-room apartment, the cats, the posters,
The drum kit in the corner, his side
Of the futon, your black bra on the high hat.

I can no longer stand beside you or take
-in your fragrance of myrrh, let alone kiss
What smoothes your lips. I have lost
My ability to hold you. If you saw
The way I look now you would no
Longer want me. Once a stranger
Gave you his umbrella when yours bent in the wind.
Once you told me stories like that, and of your childhood
Like my own near the sea. You said you felt safe inside
My arms. You said we were alike. You would not
Deny my presence in your life. Nice.

My thoughts are known to turn to her, and I clear
My throat and begin the once good song
That was the kiss from the singer's lips, the match
About to set my tongue on fire. And I turn the wheel
Along the road I am on and turn in bed to face us
When things were sweet. And I picture her hands
On the arms of the armchair beforehand—
The skyline beside her, the zodiacal light,
The smoke and all the little empties, the shampoo bottles
In the bathroom, her inexplicable nakedness,
Her skin on my own. And I sing so
Loud, pretending my lips are hers against mine
And roll down the window until every word is gone.

If for every kiss there is an un-kiss,
Must there be an un-touch, an un-breath?

They walked out in the un-night with the un-moon un-shining.

Must there be unfleshly, unfitted,
Uninhabited islands uncurled on the unfriendly horizon?

They un-left their premises untwined in the un-bed.

Must there be unlock and unzip,
Unlike and un-luck?

Their uncarved names untied in the unspoken light.

Must there be unfortunate
Un-held, unsung?

They were unsworn but unyielding when they explored until.

The way I sometimes wish to follow
Through on dark urges and the other way
Around—go into a funeral home
To have my coffin fitted, drive to
A sporting goods store and ask for
A gun to blow my fucking brains out,
Declare my lucklessness, discontent, and lack
Of religious conviction to the lunchtime
Crowd at the salad bar, max-out my statements,
Beseech pawnshops to buy my suit and rings,
Have my eyelids pierced, drink shots, smoke crack
Then get your name tattooed along my prick—
I turn into the parking lot and have my fortune told
Just to sit there in the parlor where the gypsy holds my hand.

Lively in the Twilight with Abandoning Fleas

Having observed a dead dog along the curb
A person like me concludes,
"Dead Dog, along the curb,
Modest as you are, covered
With a striped towel like a patron stretched out
On the bench of the eternal sauna,
You are not an auger of ill,
But a recognition of the end
Of one thing and beginning of another."
A person like me concludes:
"Dead Dog in the city,
Oblivious pet of women and men,
You represent our thwarted lives."
A person like me concludes,
"Dead dog, you are the ravished bride of the hour
Although I have not yet glimpsed your sex."
A person like me concludes,
"Dead dog, you are darkness's pup,
A weaned beast of life, forever absent at the teat,
Your footprints like black spots upon the tongue."
And a person like me concludes,
"Dead dog, the street was your river.
Without leash or collar,
You wait on its bank, your fur
Lively in the twilight with abandoning fleas."

The path through the grain fields looked
Real enough as he recalled the names
Of the animals. The rooster on the fence rail
Awakened the barnyard. Goats and lambs
Picked in the meadow. The sow in the pen
Looked so much like herself he laughed
Out loud as one does with a friend.

He was alone now, the way he thought
It would be, following the first length
Of trails set out by the oldest feet, through
The woods and plains to the river then across
The mountains to the marshes on the coast of Spain
Where the stars were known to go to sleep
After their work guiding pilgrims to the sea.

He was a pilgrim and a stranger, a born again
Pagan, a reveler in the vegetal gods,
Ley lines and magnetic rivers, a drinker
Of the water of ancient wells, a believer
In omphalos and phallus, a pitchforked sinner
According to the laws of the written words
Of deities supposed by modern men.

He had left what he had behind him,
Family and possessions and the recollection
Of a mouth that once answered his own,
A particular one whose lips provoked
His journey, whose words became cruel
When she said he did not listen.
When he thought of her he walked faster.

He saw a village along the river,
The towers and walls of a castle flying
The local flag. He knew there were reasons
Cities exist where you find them—
This one a low bluff at the bend of the water
Where the crossing was narrow, and a stone
Bridge built where the legions followed.

He stood on the bridge and waved at his shadow
On the river, a figure if there ever was one to
Evidence his presence. The wind drove slowly
From the east across the harvested plains. Beyond him,
Further towers and a nuclear reactor awaited.
He noted in his journal *The afternoon of the equinox*
The sky is blue as cathedral glass.

He followed the road where it turned to earth
Inside the forest where the birdsong was still
Thick in the branches though the limbs shy
Of leaves. He walked until the day was gone
And the split moon rose through the trees,
And he held his thin coat to his chest like a cloak.
The night was huge. Go this way or that was the sign.

Biographical Note

Stuart Dischell was born in Atlantic City, New Jersey. He is the author of *Good Hope Road*, *Evenings & Avenues*, and *Dig Safe*. His poetry has won awards from the National Poetry Series, the National Endowment for the Arts, the North Carolina Arts Council, and the John Simon Guggenheim Foundation. He teaches in the Master of Fine Arts Program in Creative Writing at the University of North Carolina at Greensboro.

JOHN ASHBERY
Selected Poems
Self-Portrait in a Convex Mirror

TED BERRIGAN
The Sonnets

PHILIP BOOTH
Selves

JIM CARROLL
Fear of Dreaming: The Selected
  Poems
Living at the Movies
Void of Course

ALISON HAWTHORNE DEMING
Genius Loci

CARL DENNIS
New and Selected Poems
  1974–2004
Practical Gods
Ranking the Wishes
Unknown Friends

DIANE DI PRIMA
Loba

STUART DISCHELL
Backwards Days
Dig Safe

STEPHEN DOBYNS
Mystery, So Long
Pallbearers Envying the One Who
  Rides
The Porcupine's Kisses
Velocities: New and Selected
  Poems: 1966–1992

EDWARD DORN
Way More West: New and Selected
  Poems

ROGER FANNING
Homesick

AMY GERSTLER
Crown of Weeds
Ghost Girl
Medicine
Nerve Storm

EUGENE GLORIA
Drivers at the Short-Time Motel
Hoodlum Birds

DEBORA GREGER
Desert Fathers, Uranium
  Daughters
God
Western Art

TERRANCE HAYES
Hip Logic
Wind in a Box

ROBERT HUNTER
A Box of Rain: Lyrics: 1965–1993
Sentinel and Other Poems

MARY KARR
Viper Rum

JACK KEROUAC
Book of Blues
Book of Haikus
Book of Sketches

JOANNA KLINK
Circadian

ANN LAUTERBACH
Hum
If in Time: Selected Poems,
  1975–2000
On a Stair

CORINNE LEE
PYX

PHYLLIS LEVIN
Mercury

WILLIAM LOGAN
Macbeth in Venice
Night Battle
Vain Empires
The Whispering Gallery

MICHAEL MCCLURE
Huge Dreams: San Francisco and
  Beat Poems

DAVID MELTZER
David's Copy: The Selected Poems
  of David Meltzer

CAROL MUSKE
An Octave Above Thunder
Red Trousseau

ALICE NOTLEY
Disobedience
In the Pines
Mysteries of Small Houses

LAWRENCE RAAB
The Probable World
Visible Signs: New and Selected
  Poems

BARBARA RAS
One Hidden Stuff

PATTIANN ROGERS
Generations

WILLIAM STOBB
Nervous Systems

TRYFON TOLIDES
An Almost Pure Empty Walking

STEPHANIE STRICKLAND
V: WaveSon.nets/Losing L'una

ANNE WALDMAN
Kill or Cure
Marriage: A Sentence
Structure of the World Compared
  to a Bubble

JAMES WELCH
Riding the Earthboy 40

PHILIP WHALEN
Overtime: Selected Poems

ROBERT WRIGLEY
Earthly Meditations: New and
  Selected Poems
Lives of the Animals
Reign of Snakes

MARK YAKICH
Unrelated Individuals Forming a
  Group Waiting to Cross

JOHN YAU
Borrowed Love Poems
Paradiso Diaspora

Printed in the United States
by Baker & Taylor Publisher Services